CogAT ® - 4th and 5th (
Quantitative Battery Practice Questions (Form 7, Level 10 and Level 11)

Prepare Your 4th and 5th Grader For The Cognitive Abilities Test - CogAT

By: Sam Khobragade

1) Number Analogies / Quantitative Relationships

120 Analogy Practice Questions

Grade:	4th and 5th Grade
Level:	Level 10 and Level 11
Form:	7
Battery:	Quantitative Battery
Section:	1) Number Analogies / Quantitative Relationships

By: Sam Khobragade

1) Number Analogies / Quantitative Relationships : 120 Questions

Analogy 1

[64 → 704] **[32 → 352]** **[100 → ?]**

A 1110 **B** 999 **C** 1100 **D** 1002 **E** 1108

Analogy 2

[426 → 4260] **[108 → 1080]** **[204 → ?]**

P 1835 **Q** 2042 **R** 1836 **S** 2040 **T** 2049

Analogy 3

[16 → 48] **[6 → 18]** **[10 → ?]**

A 39 **B** 22 **C** 19 **D** 30 **E** 36

Analogy 4

[132 → 1320] **[636 → 6360]** **[318 → ?]**

P 3180 **Q** 3179 **R** 3186 **S** 2860 **T** 2864

Analogy 5

[16 → 32] **[20 → 40]** **[30 → ?]**

A 28 B 60 C 30 D 67 E 59

Analogy 6

[16 → 26] **[12 → 18]** **[14 → ?]**

P 22 Q 27 R 10 S 9 T 26

Analogy 7

[354 → 348] **[180 → 174]** **[216 → ?]**

A 210 B 5 C 213 D 4 E 211

Analogy 8

[150 → 146] **[312 → 307]** **[330 → ?]**

P 4 Q 327 R 324 S 6 T 323

Analogy 9

[84 → 924] **[28 → 308]** **[76 → ?]**

A 762 **B** 846 **C** 836 **D** 844 **E** 759

Analogy 10

[18 → 34] **[10 → 18]** **[14 → ?]**

P 26 **Q** 13 **R** 30 **S** 36 **T** 11

Analogy 11

[918 → 9180] **[264 → 2640]** **[558 → ?]**

A 5587 **B** 5580 **C** 5579 **D** 5022 **E** 5023

Analogy 12

[6 → 12] **[24 → 48]** **[26 → ?]**

P 60 **Q** 24 **R** 28 **S** 52 **T** 55

Analogy 13

[360 → 356] **[378 → 373]** **[30 → ?]**

A 7 B 24 C 5 D 27 E 31

Analogy 14

[6 → 22] **[10 → 34]** **[12 → ?]**

P 45 Q 42 R 27 S 40 T 30

Analogy 15

[24 → 48] **[12 → 24]** **[28 → ?]**

A 27 B 26 C 59 D 60 E 56

Analogy 16

[378 → 379] **[138 → 140]** **[156 → ?]**

P 160 Q 2 R 168 S 4 T 159

Analogy 17

[16 → 48] **[18 → 54]** **[4 → ?]**

A 18 **B** 12 **C** 9 **D** 16 **E** 7

Analogy 18

[288 → 282] **[54 → 48]** **[294 → ?]**

P 288 **Q** 293 **R** 295 **S** 8 **T** 6

Analogy 19

[240 → 246] **[378 → 384]** **[174 → ?]**

A 8 **B** 190 **C** 180 **D** 7 **E** 181

Analogy 20

[16 → 48] **[18 → 54]** **[20 → ?]**

P 69 **Q** 42 **R** 41 **S** 60 **T** 59

Analogy 21

[114 → 102] **[84 → 72]** **[312 → ?]**

A 302 B 14 C 308 D 12 E 300

Analogy 22

[32 → 352] **[68 → 748]** **[24 → ?]**

P 264 Q 272 R 271 S 240 T 239

Analogy 23

[228 → 226] **[360 → 357]** **[108 → ?]**

A 104 B 5 C 107 D 2 E 113

Analogy 24

[84 → 924] **[28 → 308]** **[44 → ?]**

P 438 Q 484 R 492 S 490 T 441

Analogy 25

[6 → 18] **[10 → 30]** **[14 → ?]**

A 42 **B** 43 **C** 26 **D** 27 **E** 44

Analogy 26

[8 → 22] **[10 → 28]** **[14 → ?]**

P 40 **Q** 44 **R** 27 **S** 26 **T** 46

Analogy 27

[324 → 303] **[222 → 201]** **[174 → ?]**

A 162 **B** 153 **C** 160 **D** 20 **E** 22

Analogy 28

[162 → 177] **[168 → 183]** **[330 → ?]**

P 345 **Q** 15 **R** 350 **S** 14 **T** 355

Analogy 29

[336 → 342] **[150 → 156]** **[198 → ?]**

A 205 B 5 C 203 D 6 E 204

Analogy 30

[16 → 176] **[40 → 440]** **[60 → ?]**

P 668 Q 601 R 602 S 664 T 660

Analogy 31

[4 → 44] **[84 → 924]** **[88 → ?]**

A 878 B 969 C 968 D 880 E 970

Analogy 32

[84 → 82] **[396 → 393]** **[126 → ?]**

P 5 Q 121 R 130 S 122 T 4

Analogy 33

[6 → 20] **[12 → 38]** **[14 → ?]**

A 48 B 29 C 30 D 44 E 47

Analogy 34

[180 → 195] **[90 → 105]** **[252 → ?]**

P 266 Q 16 R 270 S 267 T 14

Analogy 35

[10 → 24] **[12 → 28]** **[14 → ?]**

A 16 B 32 C 42 D 18 E 41

Analogy 36

[16 → 48] **[20 → 60]** **[12 → ?]**

P 36 Q 35 R 26 S 46 T 22

Analogy 37

[816 → 8160] **[246 → 2460]** **[570 → ?]**

A 5700 B 5701 C 5131 D 5129 E 5703

Analogy 38

[120 → 102] **[90 → 72]** **[378 → ?]**

P 366 Q 19 R 17 S 367 T 360

Analogy 39

[954 → 9540] **[186 → 1860]** **[108 → ?]**

A 974 B 1085 C 973 D 1083 E 1080

Analogy 40

[20 → 38] **[10 → 18]** **[12 → ?]**

P 9 Q 24 R 22 S 21 T 12

Analogy 41

[180 → 162] **[150 → 132]** **[330 → ?]**

A 17 B 322 C 18 D 313 E 312

Analogy 42

[6 → 18] **[8 → 24]** **[14 → ?]**

P 42 Q 46 R 30 S 51 T 29

Analogy 43

[18 → 28] **[20 → 32]** **[12 → ?]**

A 5 B 16 C 18 D 2 E 20

Analogy 44

[288 → 2880] **[252 → 2520]** **[126 → ?]**

P 1134 Q 1136 R 1270 S 1260 T 1264

Analogy 45

[16 → 32] **[20 → 40]** **[14 → ?]**

A 28 **B** 36 **C** 31 **D** 14 **E** 13

Analogy 46

[816 → 8160] **[384 → 3840]** **[468 → ?]**

P 4690 **Q** 4213 **R** 4211 **S** 4680 **T** 4679

Analogy 47

[8 → 28] **[10 → 34]** **[14 → ?]**

A 46 **B** 30 **C** 34 **D** 50 **E** 47

Analogy 48

[162 → 158] **[132 → 127]** **[216 → ?]**

P 217 **Q** 6 **R** 8 **S** 210 **T** 216

Analogy 49

[16 → 22] **[10 → 10]** **[14 → ?]**

A 18 B 2 C 23 D 5 E 26

Analogy 50

[64 → 704] **[16 → 176]** **[68 → ?]**

P 678 Q 679 R 747 S 757 T 748

Analogy 51

[306 → 324] **[258 → 276]** **[204 → ?]**

A 230 B 18 C 227 D 222 E 19

Analogy 52

[276 → 277] **[36 → 38]** **[282 → ?]**

P 3 Q 288 R 295 S 285 T 1

Analogy 53

[20 → 220] **[56 → 616]** **[60 → ?]**

A 663 B 599 C 602 D 660 E 659

Analogy 54

[594 → 5940] **[486 → 4860]** **[618 → ?]**

P 6186 Q 6180 R 5562 S 6182 T 5560

Analogy 55

[16 → 24] **[12 → 16]** **[14 → ?]**

A 21 B 20 C 8 D 6 E 24

Analogy 56

[288 → 291] **[306 → 309]** **[246 → ?]**

P 1 Q 259 R 249 S 250 T 2

Analogy 57

[22 → 44] **[26 → 52]** **[10 → ?]**

A 12 B 21 C 11 D 20 E 24

Analogy 58

[6 → 20] **[8 → 26]** **[10 → ?]**

P 24 Q 32 R 41 S 31 T 23

Analogy 59

[18 → 54] **[8 → 24]** **[14 → ?]**

A 43 B 42 C 30 D 47 E 28

Analogy 60

[22 → 44] **[10 → 20]** **[12 → ?]**

P 27 Q 11 R 24 S 32 T 10

Analogy 61

[246 → 237] **[342 → 333]** **[90 → ?]**

A 89 **B** 11 **C** 8 **D** 81 **E** 88

Analogy 62

[6 → 19] **[12 → 37]** **[14 → ?]**

P 30 **Q** 27 **R** 42 **S** 43 **T** 50

Analogy 63

[4 → 12] **[8 → 24]** **[12 → ?]**

A 42 **B** 26 **C** 36 **D** 37 **E** 25

Analogy 64

[102 → 103] **[246 → 247]** **[90 → ?]**

P 3 **Q** 91 **R** 1 **S** 98 **T** 92

Analogy 65

[18 → 54] **[8 → 24]** **[12 → ?]**

A 22 **B** 44 **C** 39 **D** 25 **E** 36

Analogy 66

[294 → 2940] **[426 → 4260]** **[138 → ?]**

P 1383 **Q** 1240 **R** 1242 **S** 1385 **T** 1380

Analogy 67

[18 → 37] **[10 → 21]** **[12 → ?]**

A 15 **B** 25 **C** 24 **D** 30 **E** 13

Analogy 68

[96 → 87] **[264 → 255]** **[90 → ?]**

P 84 **Q** 7 **R** 86 **S** 81 **T** 10

Analogy 69

[864 → 8640] **[528 → 5280]** **[408 → ?]**

A 4080 B 3671 C 4088 D 4090 E 3670

Analogy 70

[24 → 48] **[26 → 52]** **[28 → ?]**

P 28 Q 66 R 56 S 27 T 58

Analogy 71

[288 → 289] **[18 → 20]** **[186 → ?]**

A 192 B 189 C 4 D 188 E 5

Analogy 72

[48 → 49] **[162 → 163]** **[168 → ?]**

P 172 Q 173 R 1 S 169 T 3

Analogy 73

[34 → 68] **[22 → 44]** **[10 → ?]**

A 9 B 29 C 19 D 8 E 20

Analogy 74

[18 → 36] **[20 → 40]** **[12 → ?]**

P 24 Q 23 R 32 S 11 T 14

Analogy 75

[8 → 20] **[10 → 26]** **[14 → ?]**

A 23 B 38 C 46 D 25 E 40

Analogy 76

[8 → 25] **[10 → 31]** **[12 → ?]**

P 41 Q 43 R 27 S 37 T 24

Analogy 77

[192 → 210] **[120 → 138]** **[42 → ?]**

A 18 B 68 C 60 D 70 E 19

Analogy 78

[32 → 352] **[8 → 88]** **[92 → ?]**

P 1020 Q 1019 R 922 S 919 T 1012

Analogy 79

[8 → 28] **[10 → 34]** **[12 → ?]**

A 26 B 40 C 28 D 46 E 39

Analogy 80

[96 → 1056] **[84 → 924]** **[72 → ?]**

P 795 Q 792 R 798 S 719 T 718

Analogy 81

[384 → 386] **[354 → 357]** **[372 → ?]**

A 378 **B** 2 **C** 386 **D** 376 **E** 3

Analogy 82

[18 → 44] **[10 → 28]** **[14 → ?]**

P 36 **Q** 22 **R** 42 **S** 21 **T** 35

Analogy 83

[84 → 80] **[132 → 127]** **[318 → ?]**

A 8 **B** 312 **C** 5 **D** 314 **E** 319

Analogy 84

[6 → 19] **[10 → 31]** **[14 → ?]**

P 46 **Q** 43 **R** 42 **S** 28 **T** 29

Analogy 85

[24 → 48] **[26 → 52]** **[14 → ?]**

A 14 **B** 28 **C** 36 **D** 13 **E** 34

Analogy 86

[306 → 314] **[198 → 207]** **[42 → ?]**

P 51 **Q** 11 **R** 58 **S** 52 **T** 10

Analogy 87

[84 → 924] **[88 → 968]** **[60 → ?]**

A 661 **B** 668 **C** 600 **D** 660 **E** 599

Analogy 88

[84 → 80] **[90 → 85]** **[30 → ?]**

P 23 **Q** 7 **R** 4 **S** 29 **T** 24

Analogy 89

[10 → 21] **[12 → 25]** **[14 → ?]**

A 15 **B** 36 **C** 13 **D** 29 **E** 34

Analogy 90

[66 → 72] **[180 → 186]** **[168 → ?]**

P 4 **Q** 6 **R** 176 **S** 183 **T** 174

Analogy 91

[306 → 324] **[324 → 342]** **[396 → ?]**

A 16 **B** 420 **C** 19 **D** 414 **E** 424

Analogy 92

[288 → 279] **[198 → 189]** **[360 → ?]**

P 358 **Q** 8 **R** 354 **S** 10 **T** 351

Analogy 93

[96 → 104] **[90 → 99]** **[108 → ?]**

A 12 B 10 C 121 D 123 E 118

Analogy 94

[18 → 54] **[10 → 30]** **[12 → ?]**

P 24 Q 39 R 35 S 26 T 36

Analogy 95

[96 → 1056] **[72 → 792]** **[92 → ?]**

A 1019 B 920 C 1020 D 918 E 1012

Analogy 96

[96 → 87] **[240 → 231]** **[180 → ?]**

P 8 Q 7 R 174 S 180 T 171

Analogy 97

[150 → 126] **[204 → 180]** **[78 → ?]**

A 58 B 24 C 56 D 54 E 25

Analogy 98

[6 → 14] **[8 → 20]** **[14 → ?]**

P 23 Q 41 R 40 S 22 T 38

Analogy 99

[912 → 9120] **[678 → 6780]** **[918 → ?]**

A 8262 B 9179 C 9180 D 9182 E 8264

Analogy 100

[180 → 165] **[198 → 183]** **[234 → ?]**

P 223 Q 14 R 228 S 16 T 219

Analogy 101

[18 → 54] **[6 → 18]** **[10 → ?]**

A 36 **B** 22 **C** 30 **D** 33 **E** 20

Analogy 102

[16 → 32] **[6 → 12]** **[24 → ?]**

P 23 **Q** 48 **R** 49 **S** 22 **T** 47

Analogy 103

[336 → 354] **[240 → 258]** **[78 → ?]**

A 19 **B** 98 **C** 16 **D** 102 **E** 96

Analogy 104

[66 → 84] **[180 → 198]** **[366 → ?]**

P 17 **Q** 391 **R** 18 **S** 384 **T** 392

Analogy 105

[336 → 354] **[306 → 324]** **[156 → ?]**

A 180 **B** 18 **C** 174 **D** 181 **E** 17

Analogy 106

[144 → 147] **[198 → 201]** **[312 → ?]**

P 315 **Q** 3 **R** 322 **S** 321 **T** 1

Analogy 107

[36 → 57] **[198 → 219]** **[78 → ?]**

A 23 **B** 100 **C** 20 **D** 99 **E** 104

Analogy 108

[18 → 44] **[12 → 32]** **[14 → ?]**

P 21 **Q** 23 **R** 39 **S** 36 **T** 38

Analogy 109

[258 → 259] **[354 → 356]** **[198 → ?]**

A 2 **B** 211 **C** 201 **D** 1 **E** 202

Analogy 110

[120 → 114] **[300 → 294]** **[174 → ?]**

P 4 **Q** 8 **R** 178 **S** 167 **T** 168

Analogy 111

[192 → 200] **[132 → 141]** **[138 → ?]**

A 154 **B** 148 **C** 147 **D** 10 **E** 8

Analogy 112

[432 → 4320] **[678 → 6780]** **[510 → ?]**

P 5100 **Q** 5101 **R** 4589 **S** 4591 **T** 5103

Analogy 113

[228 → 229] **[282 → 284]** **[348 → ?]**

A 2 **B** 353 **C** 360 **D** 3 **E** 351

Analogy 114

[144 → 142] **[138 → 135]** **[126 → ?]**

P 3 **Q** 132 **R** 122 **S** 2 **T** 128

Analogy 115

[20 → 40] **[30 → 60]** **[14 → ?]**

A 15 **B** 30 **C** 16 **D** 28 **E** 35

Analogy 116

[16 → 48] **[6 → 18]** **[8 → ?]**

P 25 **Q** 14 **R** 24 **S** 29 **T** 15

Analogy 117

[16 → 24] **[18 → 28]** **[12 → ?]**

A 25 **B** 23 **C** 4 **D** 5 **E** 16

Analogy 118

[6 → 16] **[8 → 22]** **[10 → ?]**

P 28 **Q** 35 **R** 30 **S** 16 **T** 18

Analogy 119

[144 → 138] **[18 → 11]** **[180 → ?]**

A 172 **B** 182 **C** 10 **D** 173 **E** 6

Analogy 120

[288 → 289] **[72 → 73]** **[108 → ?]**

P 3 **Q** 110 **R** 119 **S** 109 **T** 2

1) Number Analogies / Quantitative Relationships Answer Sheet

Analogy 1	A	B	C	D	E	(C) 1100	Multiply by 11.
Analogy 2	P	Q	R	S	T	(S) 2040	Multiply by 10.
Analogy 3	A	B	C	D	E	(D) 30	Multiply by 3.
Analogy 4	P	Q	R	S	T	(P) 3180	Multiply by 10.
Analogy 5	A	B	C	D	E	(B) 60	Multiply by 2.
Analogy 6	P	Q	R	S	T	(P) 22	Multiply by 2. Minus 6
Analogy 7	A	B	C	D	E	(A) 210	Minus 6
Analogy 8	P	Q	R	S	T	(R) 324	Minus 4. Then minus 5. Then minus 6
Analogy 9	A	B	C	D	E	(C) 836	Multiply by 11.
Analogy 10	P	Q	R	S	T	(P) 26	Multiply by 2. Minus 2

Analogy	Options					Answer	Explanation
Analogy 11	A	**B**	C	D	E	(B) 5580	Multiply by 10.
Analogy 12	P	Q	R	**S**	T	(S) 52	Multiply by 2.
Analogy 13	A	**B**	C	D	E	(B) 24	Minus 4. Then minus 5. Then minus 6
Analogy 14	P	Q	R	**S**	T	(S) 40	Multiply by 3. Add 4
Analogy 15	A	B	C	D	**E**	(E) 56	Multiply by 2.
Analogy 16	P	Q	R	S	**T**	(T) 159	Add 1. Then add 2. Then add 3
Analogy 17	A	**B**	C	D	E	(B) 12	Multiply by 3.
Analogy 18	**P**	Q	R	S	T	(P) 288	Minus 6
Analogy 19	A	B	**C**	D	E	(C) 180	Add 6
Analogy 20	P	Q	R	**S**	T	(S) 60	Multiply by 3.

Analogy	Options					Answer	Explanation
Analogy 21	A	B	C	D	**E**	(E) 300	Minus 12
Analogy 22	**P**	Q	R	S	T	(P) 264	Multiply by 11.
Analogy 23	**A**	B	C	D	E	(A) 104	Minus 2. Then minus 3. Then minus 4
Analogy 24	P	**Q**	R	S	T	(Q) 484	Multiply by 11.
Analogy 25	**A**	B	C	D	E	(A) 42	Multiply by 3.
Analogy 26	**P**	Q	R	S	T	(P) 40	Multiply by 3. Minus 2
Analogy 27	A	**B**	C	D	E	(B) 153	Minus 21
Analogy 28	**P**	Q	R	S	T	(P) 345	Add 15
Analogy 29	A	B	C	D	**E**	(E) 204	Add 6
Analogy 30	P	Q	R	S	**T**	(T) 660	Multiply by 11.

Analogy						Answer	Explanation
Analogy 31	A	B	**C**	D	E	(C) 968	Multiply by 11.
Analogy 32	P	Q	R	**S**	T	(S) 122	Minus 2. Then minus 3. Then minus 4
Analogy 33	A	B	C	**D**	E	(D) 44	Multiply by 3. Add 2
Analogy 34	P	Q	R	**S**	T	(S) 267	Add 15
Analogy 35	A	**B**	C	D	E	(B) 32	Multiply by 2. Add 4
Analogy 36	**P**	Q	R	S	T	(P) 36	Multiply by 3.
Analogy 37	**A**	B	C	D	E	(A) 5700	Multiply by 10.
Analogy 38	P	Q	R	S	**T**	(T) 360	Minus 18
Analogy 39	A	B	C	D	**E**	(E) 1080	Multiply by 10.
Analogy 40	P	Q	**R**	S	T	(R) 22	Multiply by 2. Minus 2

Analogy						Answer	Explanation
Analogy 41	A	B	C	D	E	(E) 312	Minus 18
Analogy 42	P	Q	R	S	T	(P) 42	Multiply by 3.
Analogy 43	A	B	C	D	E	(B) 16	Multiply by 2. Minus 8
Analogy 44	P	Q	R	S	T	(S) 1260	Multiply by 10.
Analogy 45	A	B	C	D	E	(A) 28	Multiply by 2.
Analogy 46	P	Q	R	S	T	(S) 4680	Multiply by 10.
Analogy 47	A	B	C	D	E	(A) 46	Multiply by 3. Add 4
Analogy 48	P	Q	R	S	T	(S) 210	Minus 4. Then minus 5. Then minus 6
Analogy 49	A	B	C	D	E	(A) 18	Multiply by 2. Minus 10
Analogy 50	P	Q	R	S	T	(T) 748	Multiply by 11.

Analogy 51	A	B	C	**D**	E	(D) 222	Add 18
Analogy 52	P	Q	R	**S**	T	(S) 285	Add 1. Then add 2. Then add 3
Analogy 53	A	B	C	**D**	E	(D) 660	Multiply by 11.
Analogy 54	P	**Q**	R	S	T	(Q) 6180	Multiply by 10.
Analogy 55	A	**B**	C	D	E	(B) 20	Multiply by 2. Minus 8
Analogy 56	P	Q	**R**	S	T	(R) 249	Add 3
Analogy 57	A	B	C	**D**	E	(D) 20	Multiply by 2.
Analogy 58	P	**Q**	R	S	T	(Q) 32	Multiply by 3. Add 2
Analogy 59	A	**B**	C	D	E	(B) 42	Multiply by 3.
Analogy 60	P	Q	**R**	S	T	(R) 24	Multiply by 2.

Analogy						Answer	Rule
Analogy 61	A	B	C	D	E	(D) 81	Minus 9
Analogy 62	P	Q	R	S	T	(S) 43	Multiply by 3. Add 1
Analogy 63	A	B	C	D	E	(C) 36	Multiply by 3.
Analogy 64	P	Q	R	S	T	(Q) 91	Add 1
Analogy 65	A	B	C	D	E	(E) 36	Multiply by 3.
Analogy 66	P	Q	R	S	T	(T) 1380	Multiply by 10.
Analogy 67	A	B	C	D	E	(B) 25	Multiply by 2. Add 1
Analogy 68	P	Q	R	S	T	(S) 81	Minus 9
Analogy 69	A	B	C	D	E	(A) 4080	Multiply by 10.
Analogy 70	P	Q	R	S	T	(R) 56	Multiply by 2.

Analogy 71	A	**B**	C	D	E	(B) 189	Add 1. Then add 2. Then add 3
Analogy 72	P	Q	R	**S**	T	(S) 169	Add 1
Analogy 73	A	B	C	D	**E**	(E) 20	Multiply by 2.
Analogy 74	**P**	Q	R	S	T	(P) 24	Multiply by 2.
Analogy 75	A	**B**	C	D	E	(B) 38	Multiply by 3. Minus 4
Analogy 76	P	Q	R	**S**	T	(S) 37	Multiply by 3. Add 1
Analogy 77	A	B	**C**	D	E	(C) 60	Add 18
Analogy 78	P	Q	R	S	**T**	(T) 1012	Multiply by 11.
Analogy 79	A	**B**	C	D	E	(B) 40	Multiply by 3. Add 4
Analogy 80	P	**Q**	R	S	T	(Q) 792	Multiply by 11.

Analogy						Answer	Explanation
Analogy 81	A	B	C	**D**	E	(D) 376	Add 2. Then add 3. Then add 4
Analogy 82	**P**	Q	R	S	T	(P) 36	Multiply by 2. Add 8
Analogy 83	A	**B**	C	D	E	(B) 312	Minus 4. Then minus 5. Then minus 6
Analogy 84	P	**Q**	R	S	T	(Q) 43	Multiply by 3. Add 1
Analogy 85	A	**B**	C	D	E	(B) 28	Multiply by 2.
Analogy 86	P	Q	R	**S**	T	(S) 52	Add 8. Then add 9. Then add 10
Analogy 87	A	B	C	**D**	E	(D) 660	Multiply by 11.
Analogy 88	P	Q	R	S	**T**	(T) 24	Minus 4. Then minus 5. Then minus 6
Analogy 89	A	B	C	**D**	E	(D) 29	Multiply by 2. Add 1
Analogy 90	P	Q	R	S	**T**	(T) 174	Add 6

Analogy 91	A	B	C	D	E	(D) 414	Add 18
Analogy 92	P	Q	R	S	T	(T) 351	Minus 9
Analogy 93	A	B	C	D	E	(E) 118	Add 8. Then add 9. Then add 10
Analogy 94	P	Q	R	S	T	(T) 36	Multiply by 3.
Analogy 95	A	B	C	D	E	(E) 1012	Multiply by 11.
Analogy 96	P	Q	R	S	T	(T) 171	Minus 9
Analogy 97	A	B	C	D	E	(D) 54	Minus 24
Analogy 98	P	Q	R	S	T	(T) 38	Multiply by 3. Minus 4
Analogy 99	A	B	C	D	E	(C) 9180	Multiply by 10.
Analogy 100	P	Q	R	S	T	(T) 219	Minus 15

Analogy	Options					Answer	Explanation
Analogy 101	A	B	**C**	D	E	(C) 30	Multiply by 3.
Analogy 102	P	**Q**	R	S	T	(Q) 48	Multiply by 2.
Analogy 103	A	B	C	D	**E**	(E) 96	Add 18
Analogy 104	P	Q	R	**S**	T	(S) 384	Add 18
Analogy 105	A	B	**C**	D	E	(C) 174	Add 18
Analogy 106	**P**	Q	R	S	T	(P) 315	Add 3
Analogy 107	A	B	C	**D**	E	(D) 99	Add 21
Analogy 108	P	Q	R	**S**	T	(S) 36	Multiply by 2. Add 8
Analogy 109	A	B	**C**	D	E	(C) 201	Add 1. Then add 2. Then add 3
Analogy 110	P	Q	R	S	**T**	(T) 168	Minus 6

Analogy						Answer	Explanation
Analogy 111	A	**B**	C	D	E	(B) 148	Add 8. Then add 9. Then add 10
Analogy 112	**P**	Q	R	S	T	(P) 5100	Multiply by 10.
Analogy 113	A	B	C	D	**E**	(E) 351	Add 1. Then add 2. Then add 3
Analogy 114	P	Q	**R**	S	T	(R) 122	Minus 2. Then minus 3. Then minus 4
Analogy 115	A	B	C	**D**	E	(D) 28	Multiply by 2.
Analogy 116	P	Q	**R**	S	T	(R) 24	Multiply by 3.
Analogy 117	A	B	C	D	**E**	(E) 16	Multiply by 2. Minus 8
Analogy 118	**P**	Q	R	S	T	(P) 28	Multiply by 3. Minus 2
Analogy 119	**A**	B	C	D	E	(A) 172	Minus 6. Then minus 7. Then minus 8
Analogy 120	P	Q	R	**S**	T	(S) 109	Add 1

2) Number Puzzles / Equation Building

120 Puzzle Practice Questions

Grade:	4th and 5th Grade
Level:	Level 10 and Level 11
Form:	7
Battery:	Quantitative Battery
Section:	2) Number Puzzles / Equation Building

By: Sam Khobragade

2) Number Puzzles / Equation Building : 120 Questions

Puzzle 1

22 + ? - 22 = 18 - 6

A 17 B 2 C 37 D 42 E 12

Puzzle 2

12 + 18 = ?

P 1 Q 52 R 40 S 10 T 30

Puzzle 3

26 + 8 > ? + 8 - 6

A 34 B 22 C 42 D 58 E 60

Puzzle 4

- ? = 30 - 24

= 48

P 25 Q 42 R 29 S 45 T 31

Puzzle 5

19 + ? = 0 + 10 + 10

A 1 **B** 3 **C** 7 **D** 9 **E** 11

Puzzle 6

22 - ? + 14 > 6

P 0 **Q** 20 **R** 5 **S** 8 **T** 10

Puzzle 7

? + 10 + 12 = 26 + 0

A 4 **B** 20 **C** 21 **D** 10 **E** 14

Puzzle 8

4 + 10 + 32 > ?

P 83 **Q** 22 **R** 74 **S** 76 **T** 61

Puzzle 9

42 - ? = 15

A 32 B 39 C 27 D 31 E 15

Puzzle 10

1 + 6 + ? < 8 + 28

P 32 Q 51 R 5 S 55 T 58

Puzzle 11

? > 18 + 8

A 18 B 19 C 9 D 61 E 14

Puzzle 12

? + 0 = 4 + 6 + 10

P 35 Q 20 R 5 S 22 T 47

Puzzle 13

48 - 9 = 38 + ?

A 1 B 21 C 28 D 15 E 31

Puzzle 14

39 = ? - 9

P 48 Q 65 R 20 S 4 T 69

Puzzle 15

39 - 18 = ☻ + ?

☻ = 21

A 0 B 19 C 3 D 11 E 30

Puzzle 16

? + 10 - 14 = 28 - 12

P 16 Q 18 R 20 S 9 T 11

Puzzle 17

♟ + ? = 30 - 3

♟ = 6

A 21 B 39 C 24 D 9 E 26

Puzzle 18

$? - 31 + 16 = 16 - 15$

P 16 Q 36 R 10 S 44 T 28

Puzzle 19

$4 + ? - 5 > 6$

A 3 B 5 C 6 D 7 E 14

Puzzle 20

$2 + ? + 18 < 32 + 20$

P 32 Q 49 R 53 S 6 T 39

Puzzle 21

18 = ? - 21

A 53 B 39 C 44 D 62 E 46

Puzzle 22

28 + 4 - 28 = 30 - ?

P 54 Q 6 R 26 S 11 T 14

Puzzle 23

♡ - 6 = 33 + ?

♡ = 42

A 3 B 9 C 14 D 15 E 31

Puzzle 24

2 - ? = 28 - 45 + 18

P 1 Q 17 R 21 S 7 T 24

Puzzle 25

14 + 29 + 24 > ?

A 97 B 131 C 87 D 109 E 30

Puzzle 26

26 - 24 = 14 + ? - 36

P 49 Q 1 R 2 S 38 T 24

Puzzle 27

? + 3 = 39

A 65 B 2 C 36 D 11 E 31

Puzzle 28

2 + ? < 31

P 32 Q 35 R 20 S 55 T 42

Puzzle 29

18 - ? **= 3**

A 3 B 35 C 8 D 28 E 15

Puzzle 30

42 - ☯ **=** ? **- 3**

☯ **= 15**

P 49 Q 18 R 2 S 58 T 30

Puzzle 31

36 = 24 + ?

A 32 B 33 C 3 D 12 E 15

Puzzle 32

18 - ? **= 33 - 18**

P 3 Q 5 R 24 S 10 T 11

Puzzle 33

3 = 45 - ?

[A] 48 [B] 42 [C] 59 [D] 60 [E] 31

Puzzle 34

20 - ? = 22 + 14 - 22

[P] 17 [Q] 4 [R] 6 [S] 8 [T] 24

Puzzle 35

48 - 47 = 3 - ?

[A] 2 [B] 7 [C] 25 [D] 10 [E] 30

Puzzle 36

? + 15 = ⚐ - 21

⚐ = 39

[P] 17 [Q] 3 [R] 6 [S] 29 [T] 15

Puzzle 37

30 + 3 = ♕ - ?

♕ = 45

A 18   B 20   C 12   D 29   E 14

Puzzle 38

10 + 14 = ? + 2 + 12

P 17   Q 20   R 21   S 10   T 28

Puzzle 39

24 - ? < 30

A 33   B 51   C 10   D 26   E 46

Puzzle 40

12 + 18 = 39 - ?

P 6   Q 22   R 8   S 24   T 9

Puzzle 41

18 - 6 + ? = 1 + 27

A 16 **B** 4 **C** 37 **D** 6 **E** 7

Puzzle 42

42 - ? = 9 + 21

P 17 **Q** 5 **R** 39 **S** 12 **T** 15

Puzzle 43

? - 21 = + 3

= 3

A 6 **B** 27 **C** 29 **D** 13 **E** 15

Puzzle 44

? - 18 = 39 - 12

P 48 **Q** 53 **R** 54 **S** 73 **T** 45

Puzzle 45

$$22 < ? + 2 + 12$$

A 0 B 1 C 2 D 3 E 24

Puzzle 46

$$50 > ? + 10$$

P 16 Q 77 R 46 S 78 T 63

Puzzle 47

$$? + 21 = 36$$

A 33 B 18 C 22 D 28 E 15

Puzzle 48

♜ + 12 = ? - 6

♜ = 12

P 20 Q 7 R 25 S 41 T 30

Puzzle 49

✹ + ? = 33 + 15

✹ = 15

A 33　B 34　C 57　D 63　E 31

Puzzle 50

26 - 22 + 14 = 28 - ?

P 20　Q 22　R 39　S 10　T 12

Puzzle 51

18 + ? = 42

A 37　B 39　C 24　D 25　E 26

Puzzle 52

$? + 4 < 33$

P 35　Q 22　R 54　S 41　T 45

Puzzle 53

0 + 15 = ? - 33

A 48 B 2 C 38 D 26 E 59

Puzzle 54

22 - 6 = ? - 5 + 1

P 1 Q 17 R 3 S 20 T 37

Puzzle 55

2 + ? + 14 < 8 + 43

A 48 B 35 C 4 D 55 E 47

Puzzle 56

? + 21 = 33

P 19 Q 37 R 41 S 12 T 28

Puzzle 57

20 - 4 = ? + 16 - 22

[A] 18 [B] 34 [C] 22 [D] 11 [E] 44

Puzzle 58

45 - ? = 48 - ♟

♟ = 47

[P] 35 [Q] 21 [R] 23 [S] 11 [T] 44

Puzzle 59

? + 0 = 45

[A] 68 [B] 38 [C] 7 [D] 12 [E] 45

Puzzle 60

56 > ? + 16

[P] 80 [Q] 69 [R] 57 [S] 10 [T] 78

Puzzle 61

16 + 12 - ? = 6 + 8

A 0 B 22 C 26 D 11 E 14

Puzzle 62

12 < ? + 0 + 2

P 2 Q 3 R 5 S 22 T 7

Puzzle 63

? < 20 - 10 + 18

A 33 B 51 C 55 D 8 E 43

Puzzle 64

27 = ? + 1

P 8 Q 9 R 26 S 11 T 28

Puzzle 65

45 = 42 + ?

[A] 0 [B] 18 [C] 3 [D] 7 [E] 31

Puzzle 66

0 + ? + 12 < 59 + 8

[P] 16 [Q] 96 [R] 100 [S] 106 [T] 93

Puzzle 67

☘ + 30 = ? + 15

☘ = 12

[A] 16 [B] 17 [C] 4 [D] 5 [E] 27

Puzzle 68

24 - ? = 2 + 10 + 8

[P] 4 [Q] 20 [R] 5 [S] 23 [T] 31

Puzzle 69

19 + 1 < ?

A 16　B 38　C 8　D 12　E 14

Puzzle 70

8 + 16 + 18 > ?

P 16　Q 67　R 55　S 43　T 76

Puzzle 71

24 = ? + 15

A 0　B 16　C 9　D 11　E 31

Puzzle 72

16 + 14 - ? < 24 + 12

P 32　Q 33　R 19　S 6　T 24

Puzzle 73

? < **20 + 8 + 3**

A 55 **B** 56 **C** 59 **D** 14 **E** 47

Puzzle 74

? + 8 - 30 = 6 + 2

P 33 **Q** 18 **R** 53 **S** 60 **T** 30

Puzzle 75

45 - ප = 24 - ?

ප = 44

A 50 **B** 20 **C** 53 **D** 23 **E** 43

Puzzle 76

? > **10 + 2**

P 0 **Q** 33 **R** 6 **S** 8 **T** 9

Puzzle 77

☂ + 27 = ? + 21

☂ = 0

(A) 5 (B) 6 (C) 23 (D) 7 (E) 27

Puzzle 78

33 - 30 = + ?

= 3

(P) 0 (Q) 17 (R) 2 (S) 3 (T) 27

Puzzle 79

2 + 0 + ? < 18 + 1

(A) 18 (B) 6 (C) 23 (D) 24 (E) 30

Puzzle 80

12 - 6 = 36 - ?

(P) 16 (Q) 18 (R) 8 (S) 28 (T) 30

Puzzle 81

? = 45 + 0

A 16 B 37 C 22 D 45 E 47

Puzzle 82

? - 15 = 9 + ⌂

⌂ = 21

P 54 Q 42 R 45 S 29 T 30

Puzzle 83

22 + 8 > ? + 2 + 4

A 33 B 4 C 36 D 39 E 41

Puzzle 84

27 - ? = 21

P 2 Q 5 R 6 S 14 T 30

Puzzle 85

30 > ? + 2

(A) 49 (B) 38 (C) 8 (D) 41 (E) 31

Puzzle 86

6 = 24 - ?

(P) 1 (Q) 18 (R) 36 (S) 4 (T) 13

Puzzle 87

31 + 10 > 14 + 5 + ?

(A) 32 (B) 1 (C) 36 (D) 40 (E) 44

Puzzle 88

18 + 18 = ⌂ + ?

⌂ = 12

(P) 49 (Q) 50 (R) 23 (S) 24 (T) 43

Puzzle 89

4 + 25 > 1 + ? + 7

A 32 **B** 33 **C** 2 **D** 21 **E** 39

Puzzle 90

33 = ? + 9

P 18 **Q** 35 **R** 3 **S** 24 **T** 13

Puzzle 91

9 + ? = 21

A 0 **B** 18 **C** 34 **D** 25 **E** 12

Puzzle 92

0 + 12 = 3 + ?

P 18 **Q** 3 **R** 9 **S** 11 **T** 15

Puzzle 93

3 + ? = 3

A 0 B 3 C 22 D 24 E 28

Puzzle 94

? - ♡ = 24 + 3

♡ = 3

P 16 Q 52 R 42 S 30 T 46

Puzzle 95

18 + 2 = ? - 40 + 30

A 1 B 50 C 36 D 42 E 30

Puzzle 96

? + 16 - 12 = 2 + 12

P 16 Q 23 R 10 S 26 T 31

Puzzle 97

? **+ 22 - 32 = 1 + 3**

A 19 B 37 C 6 D 39 E 14

Puzzle 98

? **> 10 + 12**

P 16 Q 1 R 8 S 42 T 14

Puzzle 99

36 - ? **= 33 - 6**

A 33 B 1 C 17 D 9 E 29

Puzzle 100

? **-** ☖ **= 24 - 21**

☖ **= 33**

P 33 Q 36 R 22 S 23 T 57

Puzzle 101

6 + 22 + 14 > ?

A 16 B 80 C 64 D 68 E 58

Puzzle 102

 + ? = **0 + 48**

= **6**

P 51 Q 53 R 70 S 56 T 42

Puzzle 103

42 = ? **+ 21**

A 0 B 21 C 26 D 11 E 46

Puzzle 104

45 > ? **+ 12**

P 38 Q 43 R 60 S 45 T 14

Puzzle 105

? - 30 = 6

A 1 B 2 C 36 D 7 E 59

Puzzle 106

30 - 29 = 24 + 8 - ?

P 16 Q 38 R 24 S 30 T 31

Puzzle 107

18 = ? + 0

A 18 B 21 C 39 D 26 E 31

Puzzle 108

13 + 6 + 16 > ?

P 52 Q 68 R 53 S 45 T 14

Puzzle 109

14 - ? + 12 = 16 - 2

A 17 **B** 37 **C** 38 **D** 12 **E** 13

Puzzle 110

? - = 8 + 1

= 33

P 1 **Q** 33 **R** 42 **S** 61 **T** 63

Puzzle 111

22 - ? + 12 < 10 + 12

A 67 **B** 56 **C** 28 **D** 60 **E** 44

Puzzle 112

0 + 2 = 22 - 46 + ?

P 34 **Q** 19 **R** 37 **S** 26 **T** 15

Puzzle 113

? - ♤ = 6 + 36

♤ = 6

A 48 B 53 C 55 D 61 E 63

Puzzle 114

39 + 22 > ? + 16 - 4

P 85 Q 92 R 14 S 78 T 63

Puzzle 115

42 - ? = ⚑ + 6

⚑ = 0

A 36 B 22 C 39 D 28 E 62

Puzzle 116

? > 6 + 12

P 33 Q 4 R 11 S 12 T 13

Puzzle 117

14 + 8 + 1 > ?

A 35 B 36 C 40 D 10 E 27

Puzzle 118

? + 3 = ⌂ - 21

⌂ = 30

P 16 Q 32 R 6 S 11 T 13

Puzzle 119

0 + ? = 39 + 9

A 48 B 34 C 72 D 40 E 76

Puzzle 120

0 + 21 = 3 + ?

P 0 Q 18 R 21 S 5 T 6

2) Number Puzzles / Equation Building Answer Sheet

Puzzle						Answer	Equation
Puzzle 1	A	B	C	D	E	(E) 12	22 + 12 - 22 < 18 - 6
Puzzle 2	P	Q	R	S	T	(T) 30	30 > 12 + 18
Puzzle 3	A	B	C	D	E	(B) 22	26 + 8 > 22 + 8 - 6
Puzzle 4	P	Q	R	S	T	(Q) 42	30 - 24 > 48 - 42
Puzzle 5	A	B	C	D	E	(A) 1	0 + 10 + 10 > 19 + 1
Puzzle 6	P	Q	R	S	T	(Q) 20	22 - 20 + 14 > 6
Puzzle 7	A	B	C	D	E	(A) 4	4 + 10 + 12 < 26 + 0
Puzzle 8	P	Q	R	S	T	(Q) 22	4 + 10 + 32 > 22
Puzzle 9	A	B	C	D	E	(C) 27	42 - 27 < 15
Puzzle 10	P	Q	R	S	T	(R) 5	1 + 6 + 5 < 8 + 28

Puzzle						Answer	Equation
Puzzle 11	A	B	C	D	E	(D) 61	61 > 18 + 8
Puzzle 12	P	Q	R	S	T	(Q) 20	4 + 6 + 10 > 20 + 0
Puzzle 13	A	B	C	D	E	(A) 1	38 + 1 > 48 - 9
Puzzle 14	P	Q	R	S	T	(P) 48	48 - 9 > 39
Puzzle 15	A	B	C	D	E	(A) 0	39 - 18 < 21 + 0
Puzzle 16	P	Q	R	S	T	(R) 20	28 - 12 > 20 + 10 - 14
Puzzle 17	A	B	C	D	E	(A) 21	30 - 3 > 6 + 21
Puzzle 18	P	Q	R	S	T	(P) 16	16 - 15 > 16 - 31 + 16
Puzzle 19	A	B	C	D	E	(E) 14	4 + 14 - 5 > 6
Puzzle 20	P	Q	R	S	T	(S) 6	2 + 6 + 18 < 32 + 20

Puzzle						Answer	Equation
Puzzle 21	A	**B**	C	D	E	(B) 39	18 < 39 - 21
Puzzle 22	P	Q	**R**	S	T	(R) 26	30 - 26 > 28 + 4 - 28
Puzzle 23	**A**	B	C	D	E	(A) 3	33 + 3 > 42 - 6
Puzzle 24	**P**	Q	R	S	T	(P) 1	28 - 45 + 18 > 2 - 1
Puzzle 25	A	B	C	D	**E**	(E) 30	14 + 29 + 24 > 30
Puzzle 26	P	Q	R	S	**T**	(T) 24	14 + 24 - 36 > 26 - 24
Puzzle 27	A	B	**C**	D	E	(C) 36	39 > 36 + 3
Puzzle 28	P	Q	**R**	S	T	(R) 20	2 + 20 < 31
Puzzle 29	A	B	C	D	**E**	(E) 15	3 > 18 - 15
Puzzle 30	P	Q	R	S	**T**	(T) 30	30 - 3 > 42 - 15

Puzzle						Answer	Equation
Puzzle 31	A	B	C	**D**	E	(D) 12	24 + 12 > 36
Puzzle 32	**P**	Q	R	S	T	(P) 3	18 - 3 < 33 - 18
Puzzle 33	A	**B**	C	D	E	(B) 42	45 - 42 > 3
Puzzle 34	P	Q	**R**	S	T	(R) 6	20 - 6 < 22 + 14 - 22
Puzzle 35	**A**	B	C	D	E	(A) 2	48 - 47 < 3 - 2
Puzzle 36	P	**Q**	R	S	T	(Q) 3	3 + 15 < 39 - 21
Puzzle 37	A	B	**C**	D	E	(C) 12	30 + 3 < 45 - 12
Puzzle 38	P	Q	R	**S**	T	(S) 10	10 + 14 < 10 + 2 + 12
Puzzle 39	A	B	**C**	D	E	(C) 10	24 - 10 < 30
Puzzle 40	P	Q	R	S	**T**	(T) 9	12 + 18 < 39 - 9

Puzzle						Answer	Equation
Puzzle 41	**A**	B	C	D	E	(A) 16	$18 - 6 + 16 < 1 + 27$
Puzzle 42	P	Q	R	**S**	T	(S) 12	$9 + 21 > 42 - 12$
Puzzle 43	A	**B**	C	D	E	(B) 27	$3 + 3 > 27 - 21$
Puzzle 44	P	Q	R	S	**T**	(T) 45	$45 - 18 < 39 - 12$
Puzzle 45	A	B	C	D	**E**	(E) 24	$22 < 24 + 2 + 12$
Puzzle 46	**P**	Q	R	S	T	(P) 16	$50 > 16 + 10$
Puzzle 47	A	B	C	D	**E**	(E) 15	$36 > 15 + 21$
Puzzle 48	P	Q	R	S	**T**	(T) 30	$30 - 6 > 12 + 12$
Puzzle 49	**A**	B	C	D	E	(A) 33	$33 + 15 > 15 + 33$
Puzzle 50	P	Q	R	**S**	T	(S) 10	$28 - 10 > 26 - 22 + 14$

Puzzle						Answer	Equation
Puzzle 51	A	B	**C**	D	E	(C) 24	42 > 18 + 24
Puzzle 52	P	**Q**	R	S	T	(Q) 22	22 + 4 < 33
Puzzle 53	**A**	B	C	D	E	(A) 48	48 - 33 > 0 + 15
Puzzle 54	P	Q	R	**S**	T	(S) 20	20 - 5 + 1 > 22 - 6
Puzzle 55	A	B	**C**	D	E	(C) 4	2 + 4 + 14 < 8 + 43
Puzzle 56	P	Q	R	**S**	T	(S) 12	12 + 21 < 33
Puzzle 57	A	B	**C**	D	E	(C) 22	22 + 16 - 22 > 20 - 4
Puzzle 58	P	Q	R	S	**T**	(T) 44	48 - 47 > 45 - 44
Puzzle 59	A	B	C	D	**E**	(E) 45	45 + 0 < 45
Puzzle 60	P	Q	R	**S**	T	(S) 10	56 > 10 + 16

Puzzle						Answer	Equation
Puzzle 61	A	B	C	D	**E**	(E) 14	6 + 8 > 16 + 12 - 14
Puzzle 62	P	Q	R	**S**	T	(S) 22	12 < 22 + 0 + 2
Puzzle 63	A	B	C	**D**	E	(D) 8	8 < 20 - 10 + 18
Puzzle 64	P	Q	**R**	S	T	(R) 26	27 < 26 + 1
Puzzle 65	A	B	**C**	D	E	(C) 3	45 < 42 + 3
Puzzle 66	**P**	Q	R	S	T	(P) 16	0 + 16 + 12 < 59 + 8
Puzzle 67	A	B	C	D	**E**	(E) 27	27 + 15 > 12 + 30
Puzzle 68	**P**	Q	R	S	T	(P) 4	24 - 4 < 2 + 10 + 8
Puzzle 69	A	**B**	C	D	E	(B) 38	19 + 1 < 38
Puzzle 70	**P**	Q	R	S	T	(P) 16	8 + 16 + 18 > 16

Puzzle						Answer	Equation
Puzzle 71	A	B	C	D	E	(C) 9	9 + 15 > 24
Puzzle 72	P	Q	R	S	T	(S) 6	16 + 14 - 6 < 24 + 12
Puzzle 73	A	B	C	D	E	(D) 14	14 < 20 + 8 + 3
Puzzle 74	P	Q	R	S	T	(T) 30	6 + 2 > 30 + 8 - 30
Puzzle 75	A	B	C	D	E	(D) 23	24 - 23 > 45 - 44
Puzzle 76	P	Q	R	S	T	(Q) 33	33 > 10 + 2
Puzzle 77	A	B	C	D	E	(B) 6	6 + 21 > 0 + 27
Puzzle 78	P	Q	R	S	T	(P) 0	33 - 30 < 3 + 0
Puzzle 79	A	B	C	D	E	(B) 6	2 + 0 + 6 < 18 + 1
Puzzle 80	P	Q	R	S	T	(T) 30	36 - 30 > 12 - 6

Puzzle						Answer	Equation
Puzzle 81	A	B	C	**D**	E	(D) 45	45 + 0 > 45
Puzzle 82	P	Q	**R**	S	T	(R) 45	9 + 21 > 45 - 15
Puzzle 83	A	**B**	C	D	E	(B) 4	22 + 8 > 4 + 2 + 4
Puzzle 84	P	Q	**R**	S	T	(R) 6	21 > 27 - 6
Puzzle 85	A	B	**C**	D	E	(C) 8	30 > 8 + 2
Puzzle 86	P	**Q**	R	S	T	(Q) 18	24 - 18 > 6
Puzzle 87	A	**B**	C	D	E	(B) 1	31 + 10 > 14 + 5 + 1
Puzzle 88	P	Q	R	**S**	T	(S) 24	18 + 18 < 12 + 24
Puzzle 89	A	B	**C**	D	E	(C) 2	4 + 25 > 1 + 2 + 7
Puzzle 90	P	Q	R	**S**	T	(S) 24	33 < 24 + 9

Puzzle						Answer	Equation
Puzzle 91	A	B	C	D	E	(E) 12	21 > 9 + 12
Puzzle 92	P	Q	R	S	T	(R) 9	0 + 12 < 3 + 9
Puzzle 93	A	B	C	D	E	(A) 0	3 > 3 + 0
Puzzle 94	P	Q	R	S	T	(S) 30	24 + 3 > 30 - 3
Puzzle 95	A	B	C	D	E	(E) 30	30 - 40 + 30 > 18 + 2
Puzzle 96	P	Q	R	S	T	(R) 10	10 + 16 - 12 < 2 + 12
Puzzle 97	A	B	C	D	E	(E) 14	14 + 22 - 32 < 1 + 3
Puzzle 98	P	Q	R	S	T	(S) 42	42 > 10 + 12
Puzzle 99	A	B	C	D	E	(D) 9	36 - 9 < 33 - 6
Puzzle 100	P	Q	R	S	T	(Q) 36	24 - 21 > 36 - 33

Puzzle						Answer	Equation
Puzzle 101	**A**	B	C	D	E	(A) 16	6 + 22 + 14 > 16
Puzzle 102	P	Q	R	S	**T**	(T) 42	6 + 42 < 0 + 48
Puzzle 103	A	**B**	C	D	E	(B) 21	42 < 21 + 21
Puzzle 104	P	Q	R	S	**T**	(T) 14	45 > 14 + 12
Puzzle 105	A	B	**C**	D	E	(C) 36	6 > 36 - 30
Puzzle 106	P	Q	R	S	**T**	(T) 31	30 - 29 < 24 + 8 - 31
Puzzle 107	**A**	B	C	D	E	(A) 18	18 + 0 > 18
Puzzle 108	P	Q	R	S	**T**	(T) 14	13 + 6 + 16 > 14
Puzzle 109	A	B	C	**D**	E	(D) 12	14 - 12 + 12 < 16 - 2
Puzzle 110	P	Q	**R**	S	T	(R) 42	8 + 1 > 42 - 33

Puzzle						Answer	Equation
Puzzle 111	A	B	**C**	D	E	(C) 28	$22 - 28 + 12 < 10 + 12$
Puzzle 112	P	Q	R	**S**	T	(S) 26	$22 - 46 + 26 > 0 + 2$
Puzzle 113	**A**	B	C	D	E	(A) 48	$6 + 36 > 48 - 6$
Puzzle 114	P	Q	**R**	S	T	(R) 14	$39 + 22 > 14 + 16 - 4$
Puzzle 115	**A**	B	C	D	E	(A) 36	$42 - 36 < 0 + 6$
Puzzle 116	**P**	Q	R	S	T	(P) 33	$33 > 6 + 12$
Puzzle 117	A	B	C	**D**	E	(D) 10	$14 + 8 + 1 > 10$
Puzzle 118	P	Q	**R**	S	T	(R) 6	$6 + 3 < 30 - 21$
Puzzle 119	**A**	B	C	D	E	(A) 48	$0 + 48 < 39 + 9$
Puzzle 120	P	**Q**	R	S	T	(Q) 18	$0 + 21 < 3 + 18$

3) Number Series

120 Series Practice Questions

Grade:	4th and 5th Grade
Level:	Level 10 and Level 11
Form:	7
Battery:	Quantitative Battery
Section:	3) Number Series

3) Number Series : 120 Questions

Series 1

84 → 85 → 87 → 90 → 94 → ?

A 108 B 105 C 93 D 99 E 100

Series 2

126 → 174 → 126 → 174 → 126 → ?

P 170 Q 165 R 174 S 181 T 184

Series 3

78 → 70 → 62 → 54 → 46 → ?

A 43 B 38 C 32 D 30 E 39

Series 4

1 → 2 → 3 → 4 → 5 → ?

P 6 Q 4 R 2 S 15 T 14

Series 5

126 → 66 → 96 → 126 → 66 → ?

[A] 106 [B] 87 [C] 103 [D] 96 [E] 102

Series 6

18 → 38 → 58 → 78 → 98 → ?

[P] 115 [Q] 112 [R] 118 [S] 116 [T] 108

Series 7

6 → 34 → 62 → 90 → 118 → ?

[A] 136 [B] 151 [C] 155 [D] 150 [E] 146

Series 8

84 → 94 → 105 → 117 → 130 → ?

[P] 135 [Q] 149 [R] 146 [S] 152 [T] 144

Series 9

162 → 246 → 204 → 162 → 246 → ?

A 204 **B** 199 **C** 209 **D** 201 **E** 203

Series 10

240 → 114 → 240 → 114 → 240 → ?

P 120 **Q** 114 **R** 104 **S** 115 **T** 109

Series 11

24 → 246 → 228 → 24 → 246 → ?

A 227 **B** 223 **C** 228 **D** 232 **E** 231

Series 12

102 → 82 → 62 → 42 → 22 → ?

P 9 **Q** 2 **R** 1 **S** 7 **T** 8

Series 13

42 → 54 → 66 → 78 → 90 → ?

A 108 B 102 C 92 D 111 E 93

Series 14

30 → 31 → 32 → 33 → 34 → ?

P 43 Q 25 R 27 S 35 T 41

Series 15

8 → 15 → 29 → 57 → 113 → ?

A 223 B 222 C 225 D 215 E 218

Series 16

36 → 42 → 49 → 57 → 66 → ?

P 84 Q 66 R 76 S 81 T 73

Series 17

6 → 26 → 46 → 66 → 86 → ?

A 115 B 110 C 100 D 106 E 101

Series 18

180 → 174 → 156 → 180 → 174 → ?

P 146 Q 148 R 159 S 156 T 157

Series 19

120 → 136 → 152 → 168 → 184 → ?

A 195 B 191 C 200 D 196 E 193

Series 20

204 → 138 → 204 → 138 → 204 → ?

P 136 Q 145 R 134 S 135 T 138

Series 21

2 → 4 → 8 → 16 → 32 → ?

[A] 70 [B] 55 [C] 72 [D] 64 [E] 65

Series 22

198 → 120 → 54 → 198 → 120 → ?

[P] 60 [Q] 63 [R] 46 [S] 49 [T] 54

Series 23

14 → 29 → 59 → 119 → 239 → ?

[A] 482 [B] 479 [C] 480 [D] 470 [E] 481

Series 24

174 → 24 → 78 → 174 → 24 → ?

[P] 74 [Q] 87 [R] 69 [S] 88 [T] 78

Series 25

54 → 82 → 110 → 138 → 166 → ?

A 197 B 185 C 203 D 194 E 191

Series 26

60 → 72 → 84 → 96 → 108 → ?

P 129 Q 112 R 126 S 120 T 123

Series 27

102 → 106 → 110 → 114 → 118 → ?

A 114 B 125 C 122 D 118 E 120

Series 28

78 → 92 → 107 → 123 → 140 → ?

P 154 Q 158 R 163 S 152 T 167

Series 29

72 → 73 → 75 → 78 → 82 → ?

A 90 **B** 80 **C** 87 **D** 79 **E** 81

Series 30

222 → 120 → 222 → 120 → 222 → ?

P 122 **Q** 127 **R** 123 **S** 124 **T** 120

Series 31

120 → 134 → 149 → 165 → 182 → ?

A 209 **B** 210 **C** 204 **D** 200 **E** 198

Series 32

4 → 9 → 19 → 39 → 79 → ?

P 169 **Q** 165 **R** 150 **S** 159 **T** 166

Series 33

54 → 55 → 56 → 57 → 58 → ?

A 53 B 49 C 65 D 62 E 59

Series 34

1 → 9 → 17 → 25 → 33 → ?

P 33 Q 41 R 39 S 42 T 49

Series 35

6 → 246 → 6 → 246 → 6 → ?

A 251 B 255 C 246 D 240 E 242

Series 36

108 → 140 → 172 → 204 → 236 → ?

P 258 Q 276 R 268 S 275 T 259

Series 37

4 → 8 → 16 → 32 → 64 → ?

[A] 123 [B] 128 [C] 134 [D] 130 [E] 136

Series 38

30 → 38 → 47 → 57 → 68 → ?

[P] 80 [Q] 75 [R] 70 [S] 86 [T] 78

Series 39

162 → 216 → 150 → 162 → 216 → ?

[A] 151 [B] 141 [C] 152 [D] 143 [E] 150

Series 40

174 → 150 → 198 → 174 → 150 → ?

[P] 198 [Q] 195 [R] 208 [S] 201 [T] 188

Series 41

60 → 222 → 96 → 60 → 222 → ?

A 96 **B** 100 **C** 90 **D** 88 **E** 98

Series 42

96 → 84 → 73 → 63 → 54 → ?

P 47 **Q** 46 **R** 54 **S** 52 **T** 48

Series 43

114 → 115 → 117 → 120 → 124 → ?

A 139 **B** 129 **C** 128 **D** 138 **E** 122

Series 44

120 → 96 → 73 → 51 → 30 → ?

P 1 **Q** 9 **R** 11 **S** 10 **T** 17

Series 45

90 → 94 → 99 → 105 → 112 → ?

[A] 120 [B] 125 [C] 113 [D] 128 [E] 118

Series 46

96 → 84 → 96 → 84 → 96 → ?

[P] 84 [Q] 88 [R] 89 [S] 74 [T] 75

Series 47

14 → 27 → 53 → 105 → 209 → ?

[A] 408 [B] 425 [C] 415 [D] 417 [E] 426

Series 48

120 → 204 → 162 → 120 → 204 → ?

[P] 162 [Q] 164 [R] 157 [S] 152 [T] 171

Series 49

150 → 216 → 216 → 150 → 216 → ?

A 213 B 209 C 216 D 223 E 211

Series 50

84 → 108 → 132 → 156 → 180 → ?

P 204 Q 194 R 212 S 202 T 198

Series 51

18 → 36 → 72 → 144 → 288 → ?

A 572 B 569 C 571 D 576 E 582

Series 52

60 → 80 → 100 → 120 → 140 → ?

P 161 Q 155 R 170 S 152 T 160

Series 53

144 → 18 → 174 → 144 → 18 → ?

A 183 B 179 C 172 D 174 E 169

Series 54

18 → 20 → 23 → 27 → 32 → ?

P 47 Q 28 R 38 S 46 T 37

Series 55

90 → 91 → 93 → 96 → 100 → ?

A 97 B 105 C 113 D 112 E 107

Series 56

20 → 39 → 77 → 153 → 305 → ?

P 616 Q 605 R 609 S 619 T 600

Series 57

204 → 126 → 204 → 126 → 204 → ?

[A] 119 [B] 126 [C] 122 [D] 128 [E] 116

Series 58

12 → 23 → 45 → 89 → 177 → ?

[P] 349 [Q] 343 [R] 353 [S] 348 [T] 363

Series 59

18 → 35 → 69 → 137 → 273 → ?

[A] 545 [B] 552 [C] 543 [D] 542 [E] 540

Series 60

120 → 54 → 120 → 54 → 120 → ?

[P] 54 [Q] 63 [R] 52 [S] 44 [T] 46

Series 61

78 → 84 → 91 → 99 → 108 → ?

[A] 112 [B] 113 [C] 114 [D] 110 [E] 118

Series 62

36 → 64 → 92 → 120 → 148 → ?

[P] 176 [Q] 183 [R] 179 [S] 168 [T] 174

Series 63

48 → 52 → 56 → 60 → 64 → ?

[A] 69 [B] 65 [C] 68 [D] 61 [E] 63

Series 64

60 → 210 → 60 → 210 → 60 → ?

[P] 208 [Q] 206 [R] 210 [S] 203 [T] 205

Series 65

96 → 106 → 117 → 129 → 142 → ?

A 149 B 161 C 146 D 157 E 156

Series 66

66 → 70 → 75 → 81 → 88 → ?

P 102 Q 93 R 103 S 98 T 96

Series 67

66 → 54 → 43 → 33 → 24 → ?

A 12 B 17 C 16 D 13 E 9

Series 68

120 → 121 → 122 → 123 → 124 → ?

P 115 Q 129 R 134 S 126 T 125

Series 69

114 → 106 → 98 → 90 → 82 → ?

[A] 78 [B] 75 [C] 70 [D] 76 [E] 74

Series 70

6 → 30 → 54 → 78 → 102 → ?

[P] 116 [Q] 118 [R] 126 [S] 125 [T] 131

Series 71

90 → 106 → 122 → 138 → 154 → ?

[A] 170 [B] 177 [C] 168 [D] 173 [E] 169

Series 72

108 → 122 → 137 → 153 → 170 → ?

[P] 180 [Q] 188 [R] 186 [S] 189 [T] 179

Series 73

72 → 64 → 56 → 48 → 40 → ?

A 26 B 32 C 38 D 40 E 25

Series 74

8 → 17 → 35 → 71 → 143 → ?

P 277 Q 287 R 296 S 278 T 279

Series 75

2 → 5 → 11 → 23 → 47 → ?

A 95 B 100 C 88 D 101 E 99

Series 76

18 → 37 → 75 → 151 → 303 → ?

P 616 Q 614 R 603 S 607 T 612

Series 77

6 → 12 → 24 → 48 → 96 → ?

A 192   B 202   C 200   D 197   E 196

Series 78

96 → 6 → 96 → 6 → 96 → ?

P 0   Q 16   R 6   S 9   T 13

Series 79

132 → 198 → 36 → 132 → 198 → ?

A 37   B 36   C 42   D 39   E 38

Series 80

10 → 19 → 37 → 73 → 145 → ?

P 289   Q 294   R 295   S 283   T 288

Series 81

198 → 12 → 198 → 12 → 198 → ?

A 5 **B** 16 **C** 14 **D** 12 **E** 15

Series 82

48 → 49 → 51 → 54 → 58 → ?

P 62 **Q** 54 **R** 58 **S** 67 **T** 63

Series 83

54 → 64 → 75 → 87 → 100 → ?

A 114 **B** 109 **C** 106 **D** 122 **E** 120

Series 84

48 → 84 → 48 → 84 → 48 → ?

P 76 **Q** 84 **R** 80 **S** 92 **T** 89

Series 85

156 → 168 → 60 → 156 → 168 → ?

A 60 **B** 59 **C** 57 **D** 63 **E** 55

Series 86

6 → 6 → 6 → 6 → 6 → ?

P 1 **Q** 3 **R** 6 **S** 2 **T** 9

Series 87

48 → 62 → 77 → 93 → 110 → ?

A 131 **B** 122 **C** 128 **D** 129 **E** 136

Series 88

228 → 174 → 228 → 174 → 228 → ?

P 165 **Q** 174 **R** 170 **S** 173 **T** 184

Series 89

96 → 128 → 160 → 192 → 224 → ?

[A] 256 [B] 261 [C] 260 [D] 258 [E] 265

Series 90

138 → 150 → 126 → 138 → 150 → ?

[P] 125 [Q] 130 [R] 128 [S] 131 [T] 126

Series 91

20 → 41 → 83 → 167 → 335 → ?

[A] 675 [B] 678 [C] 663 [D] 661 [E] 671

Series 92

120 → 148 → 176 → 204 → 232 → ?

[P] 253 [Q] 257 [R] 260 [S] 259 [T] 262

Series 93

12 → 24 → 48 → 96 → 192 → ?

A 392 B 381 C 379 D 388 E 384

Series 94

84 → 92 → 100 → 108 → 116 → ?

P 130 Q 115 R 132 S 114 T 124

Series 95

36 → 32 → 28 → 24 → 20 → ?

A 16 B 17 C 12 D 8 E 19

Series 96

78 → 86 → 95 → 105 → 116 → ?

P 121 Q 128 R 123 S 119 T 127

Series 97

1 → 168 → 132 → 1 → 168 → ?

A 136 **B** 132 **C** 130 **D** 122 **E** 137

Series 98

66 → 54 → 42 → 30 → 18 → ?

P 16 **Q** 7 **R** 6 **S** 3 **T** 1

Series 99

114 → 138 → 162 → 186 → 210 → ?

A 234 **B** 239 **C** 237 **D** 241 **E** 229

Series 100

120 → 130 → 141 → 153 → 166 → ?

P 190 **Q** 180 **R** 189 **S** 173 **T** 188

Series 101

96 → 92 → 88 → 84 → 80 → ?

[A] 69 [B] 67 [C] 73 [D] 76 [E] 83

Series 102

120 → 12 → 120 → 12 → 120 → ?

[P] 9 [Q] 22 [R] 12 [S] 16 [T] 13

Series 103

6 → 198 → 12 → 6 → 198 → ?

[A] 17 [B] 18 [C] 2 [D] 12 [E] 19

Series 104

114 → 124 → 135 → 147 → 160 → ?

[P] 174 [Q] 183 [R] 184 [S] 178 [T] 170

Series 105

84 → 90 → 97 → 105 → 114 → ?

A 127 B 121 C 116 D 124 E 119

Series 106

78 → 86 → 94 → 102 → 110 → ?

P 123 Q 118 R 110 S 111 T 115

Series 107

96 → 88 → 80 → 72 → 64 → ?

A 54 B 65 C 66 D 64 E 56

Series 108

102 → 134 → 166 → 198 → 230 → ?

P 271 Q 262 R 268 S 258 T 272

Series 109

192 → 240 → 192 → 240 → 192 → ?

[A] 241 [B] 233 [C] 231 [D] 240 [E] 246

Series 110

54 → 68 → 83 → 99 → 116 → ?

[P] 137 [Q] 143 [R] 134 [S] 130 [T] 144

Series 111

6 → 14 → 23 → 33 → 44 → ?

[A] 58 [B] 56 [C] 46 [D] 62 [E] 49

Series 112

60 → 50 → 41 → 33 → 26 → ?

[P] 20 [Q] 30 [R] 16 [S] 18 [T] 13

Series 113

72 → 78 → 85 → 93 → 102 → ?

[A] 106 [B] 112 [C] 110 [D] 122 [E] 111

Series 114

138 → 150 → 72 → 138 → 150 → ?

[P] 80 [Q] 67 [R] 76 [S] 72 [T] 81

Series 115

240 → 96 → 240 → 96 → 240 → ?

[A] 101 [B] 88 [C] 100 [D] 104 [E] 96

Series 116

144 → 204 → 144 → 204 → 144 → ?

[P] 213 [Q] 204 [R] 211 [S] 202 [T] 203

Series 117

114 → 110 → 106 → 102 → 98 → ?

[A] 94 [B] 93 [C] 99 [D] 95 [E] 88

Series 118

20 → 40 → 80 → 160 → 320 → ?

[P] 635 [Q] 633 [R] 640 [S] 630 [T] 632

Series 119

54 → 70 → 86 → 102 → 118 → ?

[A] 133 [B] 130 [C] 132 [D] 142 [E] 134

Series 120

102 → 114 → 127 → 141 → 156 → ?

[P] 171 [Q] 180 [R] 179 [S] 175 [T] 172

3) Number Series Answer Sheet

Series 1	A	B	C	**D**	E	(D) 99	Add 1. Increment by 1.
Series 2	P	Q	**R**	S	T	(R) 174	Repeat numbers [126, 174].
Series 3	A	**B**	C	D	E	(B) 38	Minus 8.
Series 4	**P**	Q	R	S	T	(P) 6	Add 1.
Series 5	A	B	C	**D**	E	(D) 96	Repeat numbers [126, 66, 96].
Series 6	P	Q	**R**	S	T	(R) 118	Add 20.
Series 7	A	B	C	D	**E**	(E) 146	Add 28.
Series 8	P	Q	R	S	**T**	(T) 144	Add 10. Increment by 1.
Series 9	**A**	B	C	D	E	(A) 204	Repeat numbers [162, 246, 204].
Series 10	P	**Q**	R	S	T	(Q) 114	Repeat numbers [240, 114].

Series						Answer	Explanation
Series 11	A	B	C	D	E	(C) 228	Repeat numbers [24, 246, 228].
Series 12	P	Q	R	S	T	(Q) 2	Minus 20.
Series 13	A	B	C	D	E	(B) 102	Add 12.
Series 14	P	Q	R	S	T	(S) 35	Add 1.
Series 15	A	B	C	D	E	(C) 225	Multipy by 2. Minus 1.
Series 16	P	Q	R	S	T	(R) 76	Add 6. Increment by 1.
Series 17	A	B	C	D	E	(D) 106	Add 20.
Series 18	P	Q	R	S	T	(S) 156	Repeat numbers [180, 174, 156].
Series 19	A	B	C	D	E	(C) 200	Add 16.
Series 20	P	Q	R	S	T	(T) 138	Repeat numbers [204, 138].

Series						Answer	Explanation
Series 21	A	B	C	D	E	(D) 64	Multipy by 2.
Series 22	P	Q	R	S	T	(T) 54	Repeat numbers [198, 120, 54].
Series 23	A	B	C	D	E	(B) 479	Multipy by 2. Add 1.
Series 24	P	Q	R	S	T	(T) 78	Repeat numbers [174, 24, 78].
Series 25	A	B	C	D	E	(D) 194	Add 28.
Series 26	P	Q	R	S	T	(S) 120	Add 12.
Series 27	A	B	C	D	E	(C) 122	Add 4.
Series 28	P	Q	R	S	T	(Q) 158	Add 14. Increment by 1.
Series 29	A	B	C	D	E	(C) 87	Add 1. Increment by 1.
Series 30	P	Q	R	S	T	(T) 120	Repeat numbers [222, 120].

Series						Answer	Explanation
Series 31	A	B	C	D	E	(D) 200	Add 14. Increment by 1.
Series 32	P	Q	R	S	T	(S) 159	Multipy by 2. Add 1.
Series 33	A	B	C	D	E	(E) 59	Add 1.
Series 34	P	Q	R	S	T	(Q) 41	Add 8.
Series 35	A	B	C	D	E	(C) 246	Repeat numbers [6, 246].
Series 36	P	Q	R	S	T	(R) 268	Add 32.
Series 37	A	B	C	D	E	(B) 128	Multipy by 2.
Series 38	P	Q	R	S	T	(P) 80	Add 8. Increment by 1.
Series 39	A	B	C	D	E	(E) 150	Repeat numbers [162, 216, 150].
Series 40	P	Q	R	S	T	(P) 198	Repeat numbers [174, 150, 198].

Series						Answer	Explanation
Series 41	**A**	B	C	D	E	(A) 96	Repeat numbers [60, 222, 96].
Series 42	P	**Q**	R	S	T	(Q) 46	Minus 12. Increment by 1.
Series 43	A	**B**	C	D	E	(B) 129	Add 1. Increment by 1.
Series 44	P	Q	R	**S**	T	(S) 10	Minus 24. Increment by 1.
Series 45	**A**	B	C	D	E	(A) 120	Add 4. Increment by 1.
Series 46	**P**	Q	R	S	T	(P) 84	Repeat numbers [96, 84].
Series 47	A	B	C	**D**	E	(D) 417	Multipy by 2. Minus 1.
Series 48	**P**	Q	R	S	T	(P) 162	Repeat numbers [120, 204, 162].
Series 49	A	B	**C**	D	E	(C) 216	Repeat numbers [150, 216, 216].
Series 50	**P**	Q	R	S	T	(P) 204	Add 24.

Series						Answer	Explanation
Series 51	A	B	C	D	E	(D) 576	Multipy by 2.
Series 52	P	Q	R	S	T	(T) 160	Add 20.
Series 53	A	B	C	D	E	(D) 174	Repeat numbers [144, 18, 174].
Series 54	P	Q	R	S	T	(R) 38	Add 2. Increment by 1.
Series 55	A	B	C	D	E	(B) 105	Add 1. Increment by 1.
Series 56	P	Q	R	S	T	(R) 609	Multipy by 2. Minus 1.
Series 57	A	B	C	D	E	(B) 126	Repeat numbers [204, 126].
Series 58	P	Q	R	S	T	(R) 353	Multipy by 2. Minus 1.
Series 59	A	B	C	D	E	(A) 545	Multipy by 2. Minus 1.
Series 60	P	Q	R	S	T	(P) 54	Repeat numbers [120, 54].

Series						Answer	Explanation
Series 61	A	B	C	D	**E**	(E) 118	Add 6. Increment by 1.
Series 62	**P**	Q	R	S	T	(P) 176	Add 28.
Series 63	A	B	**C**	D	E	(C) 68	Add 4.
Series 64	P	Q	**R**	S	T	(R) 210	Repeat numbers [60, 210].
Series 65	A	B	C	D	**E**	(E) 156	Add 10. Increment by 1.
Series 66	P	Q	R	S	**T**	(T) 96	Add 4. Increment by 1.
Series 67	A	B	**C**	D	E	(C) 16	Minus 12. Increment by 1.
Series 68	P	Q	R	S	**T**	(T) 125	Add 1.
Series 69	A	B	C	D	**E**	(E) 74	Minus 8.
Series 70	P	Q	**R**	S	T	(R) 126	Add 24.

Series						Answer	Explanation
Series 71	A	B	C	D	E	(A) 170	Add 16.
Series 72	P	Q	R	S	T	(Q) 188	Add 14. Increment by 1.
Series 73	A	B	C	D	E	(B) 32	Minus 8.
Series 74	P	Q	R	S	T	(Q) 287	Multipy by 2. Add 1.
Series 75	A	B	C	D	E	(A) 95	Multipy by 2. Add 1.
Series 76	P	Q	R	S	T	(S) 607	Multipy by 2. Add 1.
Series 77	A	B	C	D	E	(A) 192	Multipy by 2.
Series 78	P	Q	R	S	T	(R) 6	Repeat numbers [96, 6].
Series 79	A	B	C	D	E	(B) 36	Repeat numbers [132, 198, 36].
Series 80	P	Q	R	S	T	(P) 289	Multipy by 2. Minus 1.

Series						Answer	Explanation
Series 81	A	B	C	**D**	E	(D) 12	Repeat numbers [198, 12].
Series 82	P	Q	R	S	**T**	(T) 63	Add 1. Increment by 1.
Series 83	**A**	B	C	D	E	(A) 114	Add 10. Increment by 1.
Series 84	P	**Q**	R	S	T	(Q) 84	Repeat numbers [48, 84].
Series 85	**A**	B	C	D	E	(A) 60	Repeat numbers [156, 168, 60].
Series 86	P	Q	**R**	S	T	(R) 6	Repeat numbers [6, 6].
Series 87	A	B	**C**	D	E	(C) 128	Add 14. Increment by 1.
Series 88	P	**Q**	R	S	T	(Q) 174	Repeat numbers [228, 174].
Series 89	**A**	B	C	D	E	(A) 256	Add 32.
Series 90	P	Q	R	S	**T**	(T) 126	Repeat numbers [138, 150, 126].

Series						Answer	Explanation
Series 91	A	B	C	D	E	(E) 671	Multipy by 2. Add 1.
Series 92	P	Q	R	S	T	(R) 260	Add 28.
Series 93	A	B	C	D	E	(E) 384	Multipy by 2.
Series 94	P	Q	R	S	T	(T) 124	Add 8.
Series 95	A	B	C	D	E	(A) 16	Minus 4.
Series 96	P	Q	R	S	T	(Q) 128	Add 8. Increment by 1.
Series 97	A	B	C	D	E	(B) 132	Repeat numbers [1, 168, 132].
Series 98	P	Q	R	S	T	(R) 6	Minus 12.
Series 99	A	B	C	D	E	(A) 234	Add 24.
Series 100	P	Q	R	S	T	(Q) 180	Add 10. Increment by 1.

Series						Answer	Explanation
Series 101	A	B	C	D	E	(D) 76	Minus 4.
Series 102	P	Q	R	S	T	(R) 12	Repeat numbers [120, 12].
Series 103	A	B	C	D	E	(D) 12	Repeat numbers [6, 198, 12].
Series 104	P	Q	R	S	T	(P) 174	Add 10. Increment by 1.
Series 105	A	B	C	D	E	(D) 124	Add 6. Increment by 1.
Series 106	P	Q	R	S	T	(Q) 118	Add 8.
Series 107	A	B	C	D	E	(E) 56	Minus 8.
Series 108	P	Q	R	S	T	(Q) 262	Add 32.
Series 109	A	B	C	D	E	(D) 240	Repeat numbers [192, 240].
Series 110	P	Q	R	S	T	(R) 134	Add 14. Increment by 1.

Series						Answer	Explanation
Series 111	A	B	C	D	E	(B) 56	Add 8. Increment by 1.
Series 112	P	Q	R	S	T	(P) 20	Minus 10. Increment by 1.
Series 113	A	B	C	D	E	(B) 112	Add 6. Increment by 1.
Series 114	P	Q	R	S	T	(S) 72	Repeat numbers [138, 150, 72].
Series 115	A	B	C	D	E	(E) 96	Repeat numbers [240, 96].
Series 116	P	Q	R	S	T	(Q) 204	Repeat numbers [144, 204].
Series 117	A	B	C	D	E	(A) 94	Minus 4.
Series 118	P	Q	R	S	T	(R) 640	Multipy by 2.
Series 119	A	B	C	D	E	(E) 134	Add 16.
Series 120	P	Q	R	S	T	(T) 172	Add 12. Increment by 1.

Made in the USA
Las Vegas, NV
29 June 2022